CW00519743

Getting Great Results From Your Business!

A New Vision Publication from Malcolm Kilminster

Getting Great Results From Your Business!

Achieving massively larger results in
much less time – a formula for success
in business that gives you the time to
enjoy that success

II

1st Edition 2002

Malcolm Kilminster 2002

ISBN 1 85609 235 6

All rights reserved

British Library Cataloguing in Publication Data
Kilminster, Malcolm
Getting Great Results From Your Business! – 1st Ed.
1. Title
ISBN 1 85609 235 6

All rights reserved. No part of this publication may be reproduced, stored in a retrieval system, or transmitted in any form or by any means, electronic, mechanical, photocopying, recording or otherwise, without the prior permission of the copyright owner.

Whilst the principles discussed and the details given in this book are the result of careful consideration, the author cannot in any way guarantee the suitability of recommendations made in this book for individual problems or situations, and they shall not be under any legal liability of any kind of or arising out of the form or contents of this book or any error therein.

Getting Great Results From Your Business!

Malcolm Kilminster

- Use your potential
- Change your future
- Anything is possible

If you don't have time to read the book, here's a synopsis. It inevitably misses out many of the income multiplying methods contained in the text so my advice is to read the whole book.

Eighteen Steps To Success

1.   The world is changing but our values should not.
2.   In a world of virtual reality, people will want real relationships.
3.   If we give value then we have the right to income. If we give more value we have the right to more income.
4.   Entrepreneurs control the future, as an entrepreneur you can assure your financial independence.
5.   Technology is an aid to better practice, not a threat.
6.   We do not have to work five times harder to achieve five times the result.
7.   In an increasingly complex world we will all seek simplicity.
8.   Busy people don't want more information, they want less information from a source they can trust.
9.   We need to work on our business instead of constantly working in it.
10.   We can't do that unless we delegate.
11.   We need to understand the huge difference between being a 'determined one man band' and being part of a team of people with complimentary strengths.
12.   Napoleon Hill's Mastermind principle confirms that 'the sum of the whole is greater than the contribution of the individual parts.'
13.   Our methods of working need to change but our values should not.
14.   We must delegate what we are not good at to do what we know will give us our biggest pay-off.
15.   To delegate we have to 'let go of the edge', and trust our intuition and instincts to give us the result we seek.
16.   The decision to let go is usually made without the supporting evidence to prove it will work when we do let go.
17.   Winners have belief without evidence, the mediocre need evidence before they believe.
18.   Our biggest pay-off is when our unique skill is employed on our most valuable opportunity. We must reposition our business to guarantee that that happens.

Useful Resources

Readers and users of this book may find certain resources useful.
The author and publisher encourage you to photocopy and use the
following:

No other part of the text may be photocopied without the
full permission of the author and publisher.

RETICULAR ACTIVATOR

Definition
The part of the brain that collates unrelated information when a goal
has been set. It is the catalyst connecting previously unrelated
information that when combined assists in the achievement of the goal.

VI

Preface
What Does Getting Great Results From Your Business! Deliver?

Increased sales, higher quality clients, greater fulfilment and time off to enjoy the rewards of succeeding in your profession.

The contents of this book are applicable to your business if it relies upon good customer or client relationships for its success.

It is an outstandingly successful way to increase your income and achieve the higher levels of success you are seeking.

Getting Great Results From Your Business! delivers higher quality clients and customers and higher income per client meeting. It also gives you a greater sense of personal fulfilment.

It shows you how and why you should take more time off and it provides you with a personal formula for guaranteeing your financial independence plus the time to enjoy the rewards of succeeding in your profession.

It assumes you will apply a positive mental attitude and explore how setting goals in your business can energise all the components you need to bring extraordinary results.

You will profit most from **Getting Great Results From Your Business!** if you also read the reasons for setting life goals laid out in my first book **"The Sky is Not the Limit"**. I have reprinted a small part in the latter section of this book. You should read this early on to gain a clear view of the principles of personal goal setting.

Some of the goal setting principles may be new to you. Don't be put off by that. The reticular activator in your brain will make your goals come true if you focus strongly on them.

The entire method of working laid out in this book **is proven** in my own profession, financial services, and is directly transferable to all other businesses who make a living through establishing relationships with their clients or customers.

Malcolm Kilminster
August 2002

This book will ...

Explain in full the working habits you should follow

Underline the power of personal goal setting

Prove to you that the system actually works!

This book won't ...

Understand your business to the degree that you do

Do your job for you

Replace the dedication and professionalism you must apply to make any business a success

Contacting Malcolm Kilminster

Malcolm is very happy to interpret the needs of your own business on a one to one basis, he can be contacted at:

Kilminster Motivation Limited

Portland House
24 Portland Square
Bristol
BS2 8RZ
United Kingdom

Tel: 0117 942 9041
Fax: 0117 924 4486
E-Mail: motivation@kilminster.com
Web: www.kilminster.com

Contents

Yes – But Does It Work?

Here are my own results for the last twelve years. They show the scale of improvement using the "New Vision" principles.

They are directly transferable to any business that relies upon building relationships to create sales income.

Year	Turnover	% Of Sales From Top 10 Clients	Income From Top 20 Clients	% Of Sales From Top 20 Clients	Income From 10th Largest Client	Total Days Invested	Total Meetings Held	Average Size Of Sale
'89	101,455	73	93,883	92	3,076	210	174	583
'90	174,819	63	137,465	78	3,727	205	205	552
'91	301,000	57	234,540	77	10,349	200	189	1,308
'92	234,013	57	181,122	77	6,327	205	270	1,613
'93	362,000	45	244,211	67	10,893	195	364	1,244
'94	308,340	45	193,546	62	7,800	201	373	1,218
'95	491,059	37	279,619	58	13,157	184	403	1,729
'96	522,814	37	304,111	58	11,909	171	429	1,815
'97	540,545	53	379,890	73	15,556	152	350	2,195
'98	521,545	64	456,655	87	16,652	156	316	3,068
'99	564,834	60	421,154	80	20,209	125	273	4,122
'00	577,298	70	484,680	84	16,715	81	175	4,244
'01	447,120	82	403,360	90	13,256	75	181	4,609

The results show hugely increased turnover, more meetings completed in far fewer days demonstrating the increased productivity without an increased workload.

The New Vision Method

1. Set your personal business goals. These are your reasons for running!

2. Interpret the New World order and acknowledge that in the 21st Century entrepreneurs will rule the world

3. Grade your existing clients or customers

4. Locate your current top 20 clients

5. Goal set to guarantee all your top 20 clients truly offer future based opportunities

6. Work with only 20 key relationships. Massively increase the time you spend with your most valuable future based clients.

7. Provide them with legendary service

8. Take referrals only from your top 20 (This is your no cost access to new opportunities)

9. Add introducers to help you market your business

10. Delegate all tasks bar your unique talent to increase your time. (You must let go of the less important)

11. Increase your activity (see the people, sell your service)

Bibliography

I have found these books really valuable. They have assisted me in forming my views on personal goal setting, personal productivity and the 21st Century.

Books

The Power of Positive Thinking	Norman Vincent Peale
Psycho Cybernetics	Maxwell Maltz M.D.
Think And Grow Rich	Napoleon Hill
The Time Trap	R.A. Mackenzie
See You At The Top	Zig Ziglar
Time Power	Charles Hobbs
The Success System That Never Fails	W.C. Stone
Laws Of Success	Napoleon Hill
Success Through A Positive Mental Attitude	Napoleon Hill
The Great Crossover	Dan Sullivan
The Seven Habits Of Highly Effective People	Stephen Covey
Awaken The Giant Within	Anthony Robbins
Unlimited Power	Anthony Robbins
How I Raised Myself From Failure To Success In Selling	Frank Bettger
Maximum Achievement	Brian Tracy
The Road Less Travelled	Dr Scott M. Peck
The 21st Century Agent	Dan Sullivan

Audio Programmes

The Power Of Goal Setting	Paul J. Myers, Success Motivation Institute
The Future Is There For Those Who Invent It	Louis Tice, Million Dollar Round Table Proceedings
Goal Setting	Zig Ziglar
The Psychology Of Achievement	Brian Tracy
Economic Paradigms	Paul Pilzer

Thank You!

Firstly, thanks to Annie my wife for giving me the space to formulate these ideas, the encouragement to persist with them and the reason for pursuing them.

Secondly, my thanks to all the people in my profession who have freely shared their ideas with me. To name but a few, Clive Holmes, Mervyn Smith, Chris Meyers, John Mather, John Cross, Paul Etheridge, Terry O'Halloran, Barry Woolley, Tony Gordon, Peter Pond-Jones, Dougie Roberts, Keith Blundell, Dave Reynolds, Frank Weisinger, Bruce Etherington, Chris Barrow, Arnie Prentice and Norman Levine.

Thirdly, to the Million Dollar Round Table, Life Assurance Association and International Forum.

Fourthly, to two far sighted thinkers who have truly inspired me: Dan Sullivan and Paul Pilzer.

Fifthly, to the monumental authors and speakers that have made an impact on my life, Napoleon Hill, Zig Ziglar, Louis Tice, Paul J. Meyers, Anthony Robbins, Stephen Covey, Jim Rohn, Mark Hansen and Dr M. Scott Peck.

Finally to Barbara Richens, Stephen Gazard and Li Lin Cheah who helped put the book together and to Abbey Life, G.R.E and all my clients who provided me the platform for developing the ideas in this book further still.

1.

Embedded Values

"Times change but our values remain"
Malcolm Kilminster

These are beliefs I sincerely hope you share. They directly impact your ability to use **Getting Great Results From Your Business!** and multiply your results as a consequence.

They are part of a permanent value system for people in business.

There are just three:

- Firstly, you believe that success in life is earned by adding real value to other people's lives. If you give value you are entitled to income. The more value you give the more income you are entitled to.

- Secondly, there are no short cuts without consequences so you must have a deep seated desire to succeed honestly.

- Thirdly, to lead others you must think positively and **see what can be not just what is.**

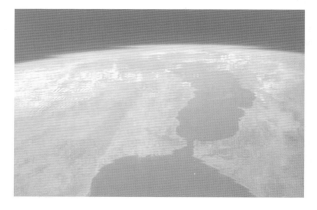

1

2.

Unlimited Wealth

"You cannot step twice into the same river"
Heraclitus

First of all – welcome! I am an entrepreneur and if you are reading this book you are too. As an entrepreneur you are part of an exclusive group of individuals who will run the world during the 21st Century.

We live in exciting times and none will be more exciting than these for entrepreneurs.

The advent of the microchip in the 1950's changed the world irreversibly.

One hundred years ago wealth was concentrated on those people who had control of large quantities of land, labour or capital or any combination of the three.

Bureaucracy governed the world and large institutions, like the dinosaurs of a bygone age, were omnipotent.

In the 1950's the computer began to have an impact on how work was done. Today, the speed of the microchip doubles every 17 months and computers now complete tasks that were previously done by large numbers of people. Bureaucracies are being replaced by microchips. White collar lay-offs in bureaucracies are faster and more frequent than the lay-offs previously seen for blue collar workers when the new technology impacted on factory processes.

Conversely, the new technology can be used to create solutions to life that in turn provide new products and services that in turn create new wealth for the creators of these products and services.

For the first time ever these new innovators, entrepreneurs, are creating wealth for themselves without much land or labour, and often without much capital.

And the opportunities don't stop there. Answers are now being found to questions posed by second, third and fourth generations of technology originally created by the microchip.

Computing power allows us to create solutions for our customers and our new economic opportunity is only limited by what technology can provide. They are no longer linked solely to our physical resources. If we innovate using computers, we can create new markets for products that do not consume old fashioned quantities of resource associated with traditional manufacturing.

For example the constant innovation in the telecommunications industry does not use much of the world's resources. A small mobile phone weighing virtually nothing is a consumer 'must have', but the value of the materials that make it up are negligible.

Technological innovation now creates markets and traditional economic theory, based on scarcity driving up prices, has gone out of the window.

Our new markets are driven by consumer demand and will create more and more wealth for anyone who becomes a successful entrepreneur. Wealth is no longer limited to those who control the resources of land, labour and capital.

There will be more millionaires in the world than we have ever seen before. We truly are entering an era of **unlimited prosperity.**

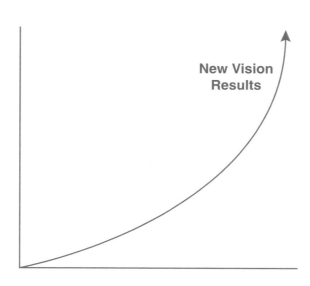

New Vision
Results

3.

Entrepreneurs Rule the World

"The future is there for those who invent it"
Louis Tice

The largest of these entrepreneurs will rule the world in the 21st Century.

Bureaucracy is diminishing in its influence and power is shifting to entrepreneurs.

The advent of the Internet is demonstrating that the world really **is** one huge global market. How many truly Communist countries are left who do not yet embrace the free market? Yet as I write this book, there still isn't one truly global company.

As the world's markets really open up and the truly global companies emerge, we will see the world's revenue controlled by those companies.

Their decisions will determine where tax revenue is created, jobs are created, and wealth donated.

Governments must and will be influenced by the power of those companies and it will take until at least 2050 for the first wave of truly global companies to be threatened by a second generation of powerful entrepreneurs.

4.

The 'S' Curve

"If I take action now I can form the future"
Ray Gilbert

This new world will create an information overload.

Choice will broaden. Traditional lines of distribution for products will be threatened or destroyed and entrepreneurs will be compelled to innovate or 'die'.

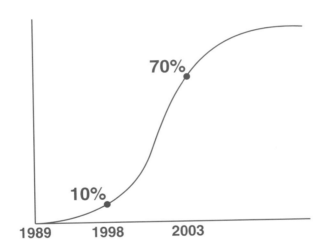

Consider the 'S' curve. This demonstrates that if it takes say **10** years for a new idea or innovation to be adopted by **10%** of the population, it takes just another 10 years for this market penetration to rise to **70%**.

The Internet was first put to work around 1993. By **1998 10%** of the urban population of the USA was on the Internet. By **2003** this will reach fully **70%**.

Could this mean that old ways of doing business will go out of the window? Yes but while methods change values do not, so we have to adapt.

The real point is our clients and our customers will have a greater choice. As a consequence, they'll experience a **choice overload.**

As an entrepreneur you too will be swamped.

This will create huge pressures on the use of your time and force you to decide more than ever before where your personal priorities lie.

The 'S' curve will compel us to innovate to keep our customers. It will also force us to decide precisely what it is we **must** do as an entrepreneur as opposed to doing what we **like** to do as an entrepreneur.

So the opportunity we have as an entrepreneur will exert huge time and choice pressures on us.

5.

So Life Can Get Out Of Balance

"Nothing endures but change"
Heraclitus

This new world will throw many entrepreneurs off balance.

Wider choice, greater prospects for financial independence, greater access to the excesses of being a success will also distract and dissipate the abilities of many entrepreneurs.

And the rate of change is accelerating. This gives you too little time to be ready and will threaten many of your traditional views on how to get things done.

This is a time to get in touch with your core values, to reaffirm what you truly believe in.

The four areas of your life you should now examine, assess and define new goals for are:

- **Your personal fulfilment**

- **Your personal relationships**

- **Achieving superb health**

- **Achieving financial independence**

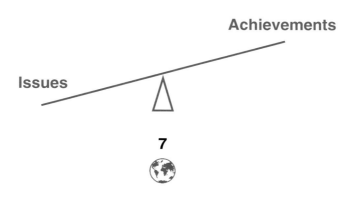

7

6.

The Only Commodity

"Today is the first day of the rest of my life"
Zig Ziglar

The only commodity we have is time, we can invest it or we can waste it.

Where we invest, it determines our income.

The personal qualities and relationship skills you bring to the business relationships you currently spend time on are entirely transferable to building other equally rewarding relationships that can lead to bigger opportunities.

The cost of processing a transaction in your business is probably the same whatever its size. You can probably treble the transaction size and not change the cost of processing it.

Would you be happy to trade some of your smaller transactions for larger ones? What impact would that have on your bottom line?

Who you spend your time with and how you spend your time in your business are yours to control. The difference in the pay-off is enormous.

7.

Quality or Quantity?

"Life becomes worth while when you have meaningful goals"
Maxwell Maltz

If you've bought this book or been given it, one of the key reasons will be because you have decided, or someone else has suggested, that you would like to multiply your results without multiplying your personal work load.

Am I right? If I am I'd appreciate your concentration on assumptions about the progress and possibilities of your business.

You **are** in business so a lot of things are going right, however:

1.   You'd be pleased if you could triple your income without tripling your workload.

2.   You probably spend a good part of your time working **in** your business and not as much as you'd like working **on** your business.

3.   You have a wide range of customers or clients and you can confirm the key facts about the types of transactions you are handling.

Effectiveness Level 1

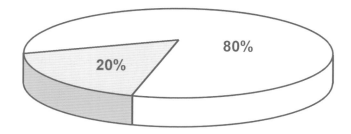

Level 1 Your probable effectiveness pre-New Vision is 20%
(no offence intended!)

8.

Cash Flow v Future Based

"When you are making a success of something it's not work. It's a way of life"
Andy Granatelli

Are you building long term permanent business relationships or just turning over money?

All the money your business receives for its goods and services drop into one of two buckets. The **cash flow** bucket or the **future based** bucket.

1. Cash Flow

2. Future Based

If at present you don't know which bucket you are filling up it will be difficult to change your business.

What you have to do now is to identify which bucket is which and then invest all of your business's time in getting money into the second bucket.

Here is a radical interpretation of the knowledge you have of your business and how you run it. It is a potentially uncomfortable read.

1. If you analysed your transactions what % of your total turnover would your top **20** clients or customers represent? It would probably be **50%.**

2. You probably spend less than 20% of each day on the things that truly matter and 80% on 'stuff'.

3. You and your organisation probably spend 60% of your time and resources handling 25% or less of your revenue.

4. The skills you personally use to complete your business transactions are transferable to others.

5. If you were forced to reduce the number of client relationships you personally handled to less than 20 in a year, you would probably ask "What do I do with the rest of my time?"

6. You've probably read about delegation and time management but never been completely confident to implement what you have learned.

7. You probably haven't set a 'day rate' for income that puts a price on the value of your personal time.

8. You are probably struggling right now to know the true answers to 1, 2 and 3 above.

Any of these touch a nerve? If they do you'll genuinely profit from the rest of this book.

The decisions I'd encourage you to make now are:

1. Analyse your client transactions and divide these into two groups – **"future based"** clients and **"cash flow"** clients.

2. Spend all of your time on developing really good relationships with **future based clients** or customers.

3. Decide what you are personally gifted at and do only that - delegate everything else.

9.

The Value of Setting Goals

"Your life can't go according to plan if you have no plan"

First, burn your budget. I'm a strong believer that a business budget gets reinterpreted as a ceiling, so set fire to your budget and let your imagination run riot. **Anything is possible!**

But to accomplish what seems to be lunatic to all around you remember:

"An entrepreneur is someone who, in possession of a unique set of facts coupled with his intuition, presses on towards a goal that many might feel is faintly ridiculous that he nonetheless knows is achievable"

Entrepreneurs have an instinctive and unique view on their ability to succeed despite those around them not in full possession of the facts potentially questioning their judgement and worth.

With a grasp of the possibilities an entrepreneur will take seemingly excessive risks if the goal is worth it.

We must set goals for our business. However, to do so we must first understand what goal setting is **and** why it works.

Think about it. We wouldn't fly with a pilot who didn't have a destination. We wouldn't play a game of football without goal posts on the field. Equally, for personal achievement to work, we must have specific destinations, meaningful objectives to achieve.

Goal setting. We set goals in the six areas of our lives:

- **Financial**
- **Business**
- **Private**
- **Social**
- **Physical**
- **Spiritual**

The good news about setting and achieving goals is that we are all goal orientated, and we all have a built in goal setting mechanism.

This is explained in detail in Chapters 35 - 42 (extracted from my book **"The Sky Is Not The Limit"**). Take time now to read these chapters.

Effectiveness Level 2

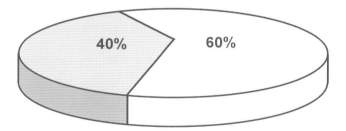

Level 2 Having clearly defined written goals in life increases your ability to make an impact on your business because you have carefully considered clear and compelling reasons to succeed, often for the first time in your adult life

10.

Belief Without Evidence

"You set the goal and then you see, you don't see then set the goal"

To succeed with New Vision we have to grasp one of the greatest principles of personal goal setting, the way the **reticular activator** works. This is defined on page VI.

Studies of goal setting have proven that the brain selects what it needs to get the job done if it knows what the job to be done is.

In other words you set the goal and then the brain starts to see solutions to the goal. It needs the goal to be set to get the reticular activator working.

The goal you select creates the task. You set that goal and then you see how to achieve it. The brain then automatically leaves **out** what it doesn't need, and automatically recognises what it **does** need to get the job done.

Setting the goal leads the brain automatically to distinguish between **valuable** information that it needs to accomplish the goal, and the rest.

In client terms, your valuable clients can be identified by analysis of your current client income.

Having "hundreds of clients" mixes the valuable clients up with the rest, usually with no reference to quality, overwhelming both your business thinking and support systems.

The sheer volume of information, obligations and client service promises you have to keep for say 500 clients obscures what is valuable amongst what is not.

"Faith is the belief in things unseen"

11.

If You Think You Can You Can

"Seize the opportunity"

We must be positive when building our business.

We adopt one of just two attitudes about everything in life. They are as opposite as **black** and **white. There is no grey.** We are either:

Positive thinkers

or

Negative thinkers

As you consider growing your business remember, **if you think you can you can. If you think you can't you can't, and whether you think you can or can't you are probably right!**

Be careful. Negative thinking is destructive. It steals the future of your business. Avoid negative people and certainly don't employ them. You can't build a business with negative thinkers.

Always hire on attitude and teach skills.

It takes longer for 10 optimists to bring up 1 pessimist than it takes for one pessimist to bring down 10 optimists.

Positive thinking asks us to see things in a certain way. We expect the best, we look for the good. Positive thinking builds our strength of conviction, it makes us stronger and helps us achieve greater things.

Positive

Negative

12.

Working On Your Business v Working In Your Business

"Always deliver more perceived value than you can take in cash value"

Michael Gerber in his great book **'The E-myth'** explains that people who get into business in a small way and succeed often find themselves trapped inside their business.

They are usually trying to do everything. After all, they built it and know everything about it. But stuck inside they can't see it clearly. Instead we need to create distance between ourselves and the business to see how we can develop it strategically.

Working on our business means getting away from the day to day tasks and deciding the strategy for our business.

The evaluation you're about to go through will help you position your business.

It will massively multiply your results without multiplying your work load!

The
Business

ON

The
Business

IN

13.

Grading Your Clients And Customers

"Distinguishing between the valuable and the rest"

This is the first **transforming technique.**

As our business grows we add people whose job is to service what we have created. What do they cost your business?

The money you spent on support is often invested indiscriminately without regard to the value of our client relationships.

I call it the "bucket of water" syndrome.

We invest the money to serve our clients and pour it evenly over our base so we find ourselves spending the same on each client irrespective of the yield they give our business.

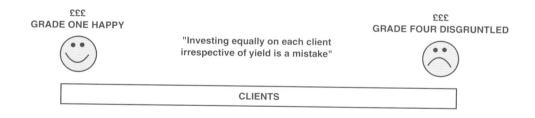

This is not only wrong, it's largely a waste of money. Why? Because we actually have **four grades** of client and each has a different value to our business.

Here are the grades.

Grade 1. High spend client or customer with good economic potential. Loves our business, spend everything they can with you. These are your Grade 1 clients who at outset will represent 10% of your client base.

Grade 2. Spend what they have with you too. Just like the Grade 1's, they always come back to you. However they have less economic potential than the Grade 1's even though they are just as loyal to your business.

Grade 3. Could have excellent or economic potential but they don't see you as their sole supplier. They don't have the closeness of relationship with you that you'd like. They see you as one of their sources of supply not their sole supplier. Probably only have bought once.

Grade 4. Could also have excellent or modest economic potential. Bought once from you, wouldn't buy again. Can't stand your firm! Don't want to deal with you, but you keep mailing them hoping for a result because you think you ought to do so. No result is possible.

The bucket of water is the money spent indiscriminately on serving all four grades equally without thought to their economic potential, actual yield or relationship with you.

This approach is typical **and** it's a waste of money.

Effectiveness Level 3

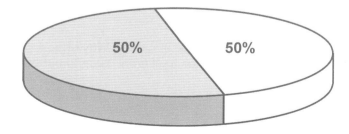

Level 3 Grade your clients so that your time is spent on your best value opportunities

19

Here's how we manage the four grades.

1. Identify your **Grade 1's** and double your frequency of face to face activity with them. Intensify your service, invest more of your resources on them, create client delight.

2. **Grade 2's.** Half the frequency of contact as Grade 1's. Make them realise they are a core client of yours.

3. **Grade 3's.** You have two choices. You should treat them now as if they were brand new clients and try to recreate a positive relationship which elevates their view of your business to that of a Grade 1 or 2 client. Try particularly hard with those whose economic potential makes it clear they could be a Grade 1 client. Alternatively if you've no time to do this, put them on a 'mail order' basis if that's possible so that they are getting greater attention from you.

4. **Your Grade 4's. Close these files!** If you haven't the nerve to do this establish minimum frequency of contact but you'll probably be wasting your money! Your other option is to hand these files to someone who hasn't dealt with them before to see if they can create a rapport with them and revise the relationship.

The point of all this? Your clients' value is linked first to the strength of their relationship with you and secondly to their economic potential.

It's the quality of the relationship that will unlock their economic potential to your business not their economic value alone. If they are wealthy but can't stand you how can they be valuable to you?

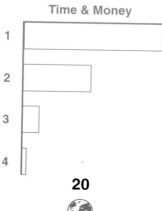

Time & Money

20

14.

Locating Your Top Twenty Clients Or Customers – 'A' Book System

"Why do I rob banks? That's where the money is!"
Willie Sutton

It's now time to take your client grading one step further. Here is the second totally transforming technique. You will need to analyse your customer transactions for the last 12 months to use it.

Working for a range of clients every year over a twelve year period I have discovered 20 "Future based"[*] clients are key to your long term prosperity.

•   If you transact business with **100** clients in a year the top **20** will give you **50%** of your income

•   If you transact business with **200** clients in a year the top **20** will give you **50%** of your income

•   If you transact business with **300** clients in a year the top **20** will give you **50%** of your income

If you have at least 20 clients you can truly say are **Grade 1's,** (the best of your best), that are truly "future based", (that is growing, expanding and continually seeking your services) you have the foundations of a long term profitable client base.

The goal is to have 20 future based Grade 1 client relationships. The emphasis is on the words "future based".

This top 20 are your 1A's. "Cross sell" them with everything possible. **See them 4 to 6 times a year,** bombard them with **superb service.** These are the only clients you ask to refer you.

Like attracts like and the referrals from your **Top 20** will be the best you will ever receive.

Revise your **Top 20** list every **90** or **180** days. Check your income from your clients for the past **90** or **180** days and with that reset your **Top 20** list.

This will add more people to your **Top 20** list but as you will see later delegation removes the problem of maintaining service to these people too.

Your top 20 clients receive five star treatment. **You must give maximum service. Quadruple your activity** with these clients.

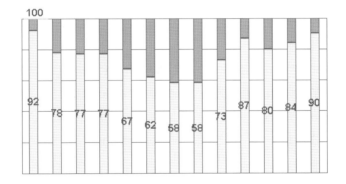

% of income obtained over 13 years every year from my Top 20 clients

* **Future based.** Growing, in need of continual servce, long term economic potential, always is motion and likely to succeed in the future.

15.

Must Give Maximum Service

"Little hinges swing big doors"

So now your activity pattern on your clients and customers shifts from the "bucket of water" system (treating them all the same irrespective of economic yield) to a tiered activity and service pattern.

This pattern is based on three criteria:

> The quality of the relationship with the client
>
> The economic potential of the client
>
> The amount they are spending with you

The activity pattern is:

Your top 20	Four times the service and attention
Grade 1	Twice the service and attention
Grade 2	Good quality service
Grade 3	See again, win them back to Grade 2 or add to mailing database
Grade 4	Close or, if you must, minimal activity

16.

Goal Setting To Find Your Top 20 Clients

*"Progress always involves risk, you cannot steal second base
and keep your foot on first"*
Frederick Wilson

So having done the analysis, do all your **current** top 20 clients or customers, based on their 'spend' over a year with your business, really excite you as future based clients? Or are some often not really future based opportunities?

Be absolutely truthful because this judgement really matters.

Most of us will end up with a top 20 for the last 12 months where probably **12-15** are truly future based. So maybe we don't have 20 key relationships at this point.

How do we get 20 future based clients?

Paul J. Meyers says in his brilliant audio tape **"The Power of Goal Setting"** that he took a bet for **$5,000** back in 1970 that if he hung an empty bird cage in his hall he'd **never** buy a bird.

Day by day he'd walk past the bird cage as he left for work and within a year he relented and bought a bird, losing $5,000 in the process.

Why? Because the space in the bird cage, the gap, drove him to fill it.

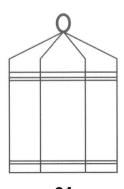

24

You can goal set to find your ideal clients in this way too.

Apply the principles of goal setting to locating your **Top 20.** Goal setting actually works!

Firstly, list all the clients you believe to be good enough to form part of your future based **Top 20.** They should all be future based entrepreneurial clients. If you only have **11,** by keeping your list in sight, the reticular activator in the brain will automatically focus on finding the other **9.**

So, the goal is **20**, you have **11**, and the **9** gaps drives you to locate the **9** you need.

The process of listing harnesses your conscious and subconscious mind to find the **20** people you need.

Remember, at the outset the clients listed can only be part of your **Top 20** if they've **bought from you in the last 12 months** and the income you've derived from them puts them in your **Top 20**.

List them in descending order.

If all your **Top 20** clients are Grade 1 they alone will lead you to further high quality income clients as they refer you to others.

Effectiveness Level 4

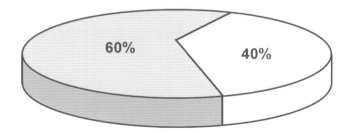

Level 4 Using goal setting as a method of locating the other clients you need increases your effectiveness further still!

The Top Twenty Client List

No.	Name	£ Value
1		
2		
3		
4		
5		
6		
7		
8		
9		
10		
11		
12		
13		
14		
15		
16		
17		
18		
19		
20		

17.

Relationships - Creating Customer Delight

"Put all you have into all you do"
Andrew Matthews

Serving your **Top 20** clients well develops long lasting relationships with them. These Top 20 will provide recommendations to others that will in turn add new Grade 1 clients.

Your Top 20 clients are your long term sales force. These are the clients that will refer you, come back to you again and again, and year in year out give you at least **50%** of your business's annual income.

To keep them working hard for you, you need to remind them that you are around!

Decide on the exceptional levels of service you will offer and start providing it. Use all your business resources to serve these **twenty clients really well.**

In my own business our Top 20 list is headed **"must give maximum service".** It lists the names of all the twenty clients we are giving exceptional service to.

Customer satisfaction is not enough. We have to aim to **delight** customers and create an indispensable relationship with our customers and clients.

Effectiveness Level 5

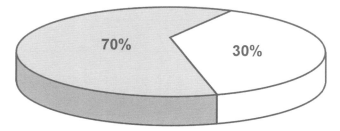

Level 5 Working on your top 20 4x a year will leverage your personal impact on your results even more!

18.

So Exactly What Is Your Talent?

"There's no greater burden than an unrealised potential"
Snoopy

To get 20 clients on side and delighted you've got to explain things their way.

There's a saying:

"They are all smart enough if you're good enough."

It actually refers to teaching but can be paraphrased to:

"They'll all be delighted if you do what it takes to delight them."

So how many times do you try to delight a top 20 client? **As many as it takes!**

What value are you providing your client with? What do you do that distinguishes you from the rest? What is it that enables you to win this sort of client to you permanently?

1.   They buy from you so they must **trust** you.

2.   They clearly **relate** very well to you.

These two elements, **relationship and trust** tally with Dan Sullivan's thinking in The Strategic Coach Programme.

These 20 core clients trust you and relate to you. It's that that gives them the confidence to come back to you and refer you on to others.

Your particular talent is the ability to build a life long relationship and instil trust in you and your services.

So to be totally productive you need to spend all of your time doing this. Everything else can and should be delegated.

In the end, you often just have to be there for a transaction to go ahead.

Now you've created strong relationships with **20 Grade 1 future based clients.** What do you do next?

19.

Sixty Superb Referrals

"I've never been able to equal the results I get with referred leads"
Dale E. Walts

Now you have your list of **20** future based clients. You are spending the majority of your relationship building time with these clients. You are seeing them at least **4** times and possibly **6** times a year.

They feel important and they love the service you give them and they've the economic potential to be future based entrepreneurs.

How do you get another 60 just like them? Simple, just ask each of your top 20 clients for 3 recommendations or referrals.

Ask your top 20 clients who they know is a future based entrepreneur that you would be likely to get on with.

This must become a specific part of your business practice.

The simplest way to do this is often to add the word "recommendation" to your client meeting agenda.

Do you use agendas for your client meetings? Do so and always put **"Recommendations"** on your agenda. You then have the option to ask for a recommendation every time you sit with a Top 20 client.

Sixty Superb Referrals

Client	Referral 1	Referral 2	Referral 3
1			
2			
3			
4			
5			
6			
7			
8			
9			
10			
11			
12			
13			
14			
15			
16			
17			
18			
19			
20			

This may seem a deceptively simple technique, but I've rarely been able to match the income I gain from a quality referral **of the right** quality.

How do you get them?

To guarantee **60**, list your **top 20** clients using the table in this section. Write in all the referrals you've already obtained from your **top 20** clients. The gaps in your table, **60** superb referrals, just like the bird missing from the bird cage, will drive you.

Remember you set the goal and then you see. Your goal is **60** superb referrals. You can't miss if you set the goal because the subconscious **will** be asking the question continually if you set it up to do so.

The **60** spaces will drive you consciously and subconsciously to fill them.

20.

Beyond Sixty Referrals – Introducers

"Turn prospecting into a procedure so that it no longer becomes a problem"
Ben Feldman

The saying goes **"It's not what you know but who you know!"**

It goes one step further. **"It's not who you know, it's what you do with who you know that really matters!"**

Introducers give you access immediately to other quality clients. They save you prospecting time and properly position you with the right quality of client **now**.

List 10 people now, that you know, who you believe could give you good quality introductions.

A number of them, if not all of these, will be your clients, or professional connections such as bank, accounting or legal contacts. Some could be secretaries, chairpersons or leading figures in business, sport, social or church organisations.

Another source of introductions can often be a professional person who has now retired. They know a good many people, have time to spare, want to use their brains and are usually keen to supplement their income.

Communicating
I recommend you distribute a circular on key issues for your introducers, sending it out say once a quarter. This will alert them to opportunities they may care to mention to prospective clients on your behalf.

Goal Setting Your Introducers
If you don't have introducers right now, use the introducer table attached to programme your subconscious to locate them.

Goal setting really works! Your **10** gaps will drive you both consciously and subconsciously to find these people.

Top Ten Ideal Introducers

Name	Telephone Number	Professional Position	Comments
1			
2			
3			
4			
5			
6			
7			
8			
9			
10			

21.

Distinguishing Between The Valuable And the Rest

"Think and grow rich"
Napoleon Hill

So now you've got your personal activity and your business's activity based around a core of **20** future based clients that's renewed and reviewed as new significant results occur.

All 20 of these clients are future based. You are also getting **60** superb referrals and to give you other opportunities you now have **10** introducers who will help you build your business.

Now you find you're overworked! What are you going to do?

It's now time to decide what only you alone have to do within your organisation. What is it that you are **uniquely gifted at?**

Just what is your particular ability? What's the reason that your clients or customers often only want to deal with you?

Once you know the answer to this question you can delegate the rest.

Accelerated results now come from empowering other people to get done those things that otherwise get bottlenecked with you.

I find many business people will reply to this by saying they are a skilled engineer or skilled with numbers but that's not the answer we're looking for here.

What we're looking for is your **unique** ingredient.

If you asked your clients and staff what your unique ability was, what would they say?

If you are succeeding with your clients your unique skill has probably been the ability to build trust and create a lasting relationship with them.

Everything else is capable of being delegated to someone else who can do it as well as you or perhaps better than you.

Every delegation creates extra time for you. The time found thus allows you the space to ponder and pursue your larger goals.

To multiply your productivity you have to learn to distinguish between the valuable and the rest. Retain the valuable and delegate the rest.

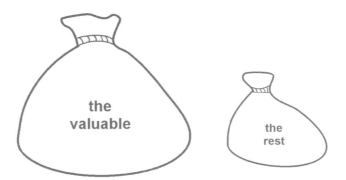

22.

Getting Rid Of 'The Rest' By Delegating

"Delegation is the most powerful tool leaders have"

Make a list of every facet of your business. Put yourself in the centre of the page.

Put every task around you like the spokes of a wheel in the order that your business follows.

Then highlight the things that only you **must do.**

Look again. Ask how can I give those things away? What would it cost me? What extra time would I gain?

Could I use the time I win back more profitably to build the business further?

Create a space in time to work on your business, separate the wood from the trees. Decide what only you can do, delegate the rest.

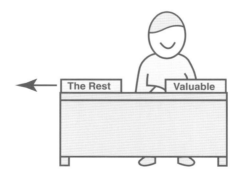

23.

So Why We Don't Delegate?

*"Multiply our results through using other people's skills
to help us do better with clients"*
Malcolm Kilminster

1.   **"It takes so long to explain that it's quicker to do it myself."**

     This time but not the next time or the time after.

2.   **"I don't trust them to do it correctly."**

     Have you got the right staff in place?

3.   **"I want to stay in control."**

     Yes, but what should you be doing?

4.   **"But I like doing this."**

     A fundamental truth not often admitted, but is it the job you should be doing?

5.   **"They are not as good as me."**

     Yes, possibly at this moment, but the freedom you gain if they do it instead of you will multiply your productivity two, three, four, five fold.

24.

Creating A Superb Support Team

"Doing the right thing is never wrong"
Brain R Beveridge, CLU

Use the planner adjacent to decide what you should retain and what you should delegate. Use A3 paper. Give yourself plenty of room to be creative and note in detail all the tasks you are going to delegate.

Don't worry about the cost, just set out the tasks. The costs will take care of themselves. **Just do it.**

Effectiveness Level 6

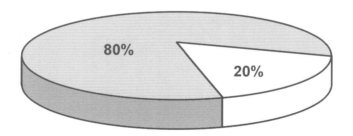

Level 6 Delegating all non-unique tasks to a gifted support team gives you back time to spend with your best opportunities. Now you're flying!

Your Unique Method

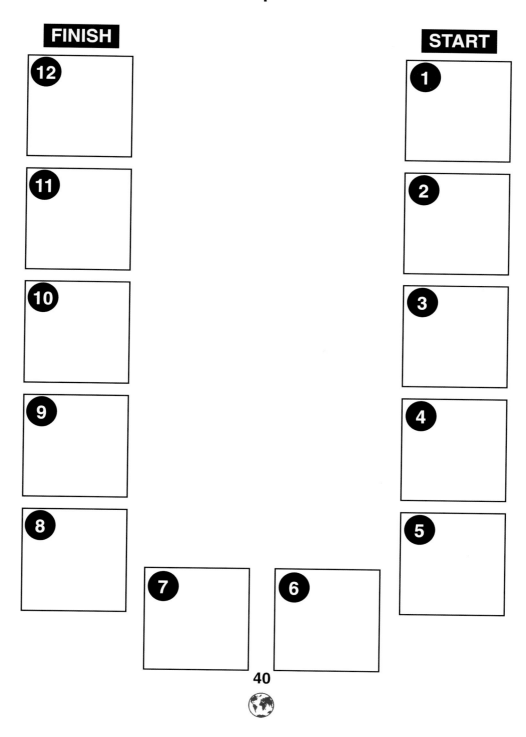

25.

Letting Go!

"Our two heads are better than my one"

Many people reading this will be finding it hard to let go of the functions they've created when building their own business.

That's only natural. It's their 'baby' and they know that they know best how to carry out most of the tasks in their business.

The first question we should be asking though is, **"What is the most we can achieve as a business if we keep control of everything ourselves?"**

The second question is, **"If I do keep control of everything what does it cost me personally?"**

Long hours, fatigue, diminished performance, no time off to rejuvenate, an above average income, no time to spend it! Fractured and damaged relationships with the ones we love and on and on.

We will only give away what we are convinced we are best at if we will also acknowledge that by dividing our role with someone else they may not do it as well as us **but** it frees us up to do other more important things.

It's not the other people around us being perfect (we're not), it's about other people being productive even if they are only **70%** as effective as we would have been because it's the letting go that allows us free time to work **on** our business.

The analogy that comes to mind is you can 'busk' it as a one man band or be the conductor of an orchestra. They're both playing your tune. Which one sounds better?

41

26.

Are Your Staff A Cost?

"Individualism wins trophies but teamwork wins pennants"

No, you must see your staff as an investment, not a cost. When you see staff as an investment you'll be willing to invest to multiply the result. Your staff are most definitely an investment. They free you to build and develop the bigger picture as long as there is a profitable outcome from each function performed.

Are your staff a cost or an investment?

27.

Building A Winning Team

"Getting things done through others"

The Rules

1. Unless you want to replicate you in every respect don't recruit in your own image.

2. Find people who can carry out the specialised tasks you've identified to increase your business output.

3. Profile them by using a psychological test* to see what their working style is like. The profile measures:

   D   **Ability to influence others**
   I   **Dominance v being dominated**
   S   **Steadiness (being task oriented) v hyperactive**
   C   **Compliance (ability to follow your instructions) v being non-compliant**

   Most people interview quite well. They say what you want to hear. They don't always reveal the characteristics they'll display day to day in the job so profiling them is essential.

4. Victor Hugo said, "Men have foresight but women have insight." Trust female intuition, seek female opinions.

5. Telephone all referees and ask the person they actually worked for how they performed. Reference letters can be deceptive.

6. Make every offer conditional upon a trial period at the end of which you both reflect on their progress.

7. Don't expect to be right every time but don't be cynical about people - they look to you for leadership, reassurance and encouragement.

8. You don't pay staff with counterfeit money so you've the right to ensure you are not getting counterfeit results.

* I am happy to supply the profiling system.

43

28.

The Mastermind Principle

"How big we think determines the size of our accomplishments"

Napoleon Hill's great book **'Think and Grow Rich'** the definitive book on personal achievement in the 20th Century explains that whenever a group of people come together with a common goal in mind the whole is greater than the sum of the individual parts.

When we are building our team we need to see how each team member can leverage a larger result for the business by being part of a team. What impact does a team member bring to bear on multiplying the results of the company?

Here's an illustration of team work in action.

If each of your team operates independently of the others, with no thought to how they impact on the effect results of the business, the result may well look like this:

$$2 + 2 + 2 + 2 + 2 = 10$$

Get the team working together to multiply the outcome and you could be getting this result instead:

$$2 \times 2 \times 2 \times 2 \times 2 = 32$$

Same people, different leverage and a massive rise in results because each person is pulling in the same direction for the common good!

29.

The New Vision Principles

"Spend 80% of your time on your most promising opportunities"

There are ten "must dos" or "must knows" to breakthrough to the massively better results you seek. These are:

1. Understand the principles of goal setting and then use goal setting as an everyday technique in your business.

2. Grade your clients.

3. Analyse your company's income and locate your top 20 sources of income.

4. Edit these to locate which of the **20** are potential or actual future based long term trading opportunities. These 20 clients must be giving you or be capable of giving you the highest income of all your clients **and** to be leading you to others just like them.

5. If you don't have 20 future based clients of the right quality goal set to find the others.

6. Increase your activity around these 20 clients. Give maximum service to create customer delight.

7. Ask each of these **20** clients for 3 superb recommendations.

8. Build an team of introducers to add more quality clients into your business.

9. Define your indispensible and unique talents within your own business. **Delegate everything else.** Build an orchestra, don't be a one man band. It doesn't sound the same and you run out of energy playing all those instruments yourself.

10. Set meaningful goals for your business so that you and your team are motivated to get the best possible results.

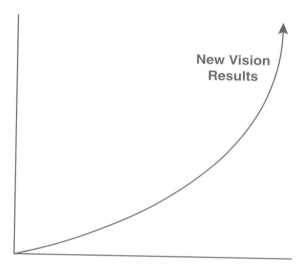

New Vision
Results

30.

Entrepreneurial Tools

"Every day you write your own pay cheque"

1.   Goal setting in your diary - getting more done each week

Most people write appointments in their diary as they occur. Change to the goal setting diary system. Lay out your ideal meeting pattern defining when you would like your meetings to take place.

Now as you look at your week you'll see the 10, 12 or 20 spaces waiting to be filled. The sub-conscious mind now starts trying to fill the gaps you've created.

BEFORE

Mon	Tue	Wed	Thu	Fri
Jones	Brown		Watson	

AFTER

Mon	Tue	Wed	Thu	Fri
9 Jones	9 Smith	9 Bloggs	9	9 James
11 Brown	11 Simpson	11	11 Clarke	11
1	1	1	1 Stevens	1 Mills
3	3 Watson	3 James	3	3
5	5	5 Holmes	5 Tompson	5

Confirming again how it works

a. Put your ideal activity pattern on each page at the times you want them.

b. The empty spaces create the momentum.

c. Each line needs a name on it.

d. You will naturally activate your inbuilt goal setting ability to fill in the gaps.

The alternative, leaving the pages blank, and getting excited whenever you fill in one name on any page does not deliver in the same way. You always underperform.

2. Colour coding your activities

Work in colour. It **really** works.

Walt Disney worked in colour when problem solving. Specific colours stimulate specific responses. Use different colours for different diary entries.

Use four colours to enter your daily appointments in your diary, your lists of work to do, your calls to make, and the people you are seeing. Each has a different commercial value and relevance and the brain responds to the stimulus of colour.

blue	**for new client meeting**
red	**for money generating meetings**
green	**for client service meetings**
black	**for non income generating activities**

These colours give each activity a "value" according to the revenue potential of each of them and it utilises your inbuilt goal setting mechanism making you respond differently to the "values" of each type of meeting.

3. Using a psychological profile to know how your staff will perform

I profile all applicants using the Insight Personality Inventory (IPI). My experience is that people interview one way and operate another. As a consequence you're rarely interviewing the real person. The IPI measures four traits. These are:

D	**Dominance**
I	**Influence**
S	**Steadiness**
C	**Compliance**

Once marked it shows you:

    a.   Their projected view of their behavioural style

    b.   How they actually behave away from workplace pressure

    c.   How they are actually likely to function at work

By interpreting people's working styles you can avoid conflict and understand what to really expect from someone when they start working for you.

There are no right or wrong answers and the IPI is a valuable indicator of a person's working style, what they'll be comfortable doing and what they'd rather avoid doing in their working environment.

Absolutely invaluable. Nobody joins us without this first being completed and analysed.

We will happily profile one of your key people to see how they will operate in your business.

4.   Goal setting the gaps

This is Paul J. Meyer's birdcage again. The 'gap' in the birdcage drove him to fill it by buying a bird even though he bet $5000 if he hung a birdcage empty in his hall he'd **never** buy a bird. He lost his bet.

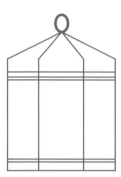

Use this for your Top 20 client relationships, your 60 superb referrals, your Top 10 Introducers and your diary layout. The gaps will drive your subconscious to compute solutions to the questions you pose it.

An example:

Are you currently looking for extra sales staff? Do you have a manpower objective? Are you planning on adding say 10 new future based clients, or perhaps 10 introducers?

Try using a whiteboard and boxes.

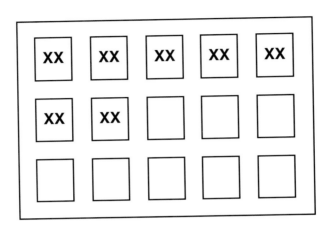

Say this is your whiteboard. You've **15** boxes with **7** filled. This leaves **8** left empty.

Your subconscious will continually ask the question "where will I find the other **8** people" as long as it's recorded. To stimulate your subconscious part put the whiteboard where you will see it each day. The high visibility will continually bring the subconscious back to the question, "Where will I find the other **8** people for my team?"

The **8** gaps will drive you even when you're **not** consciously thinking about them.

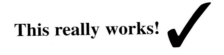

This really works!

5.   Setting and Recording Sales Objectives

Use a graph. This sounds simple, even silly but this really works. Chart the ideal course, track it weekly/daily. Make it prominent so that it can't be ignored. The graph motivates you to complete it.

The visual impact of this simple graph is staggering. **It too only works!**

The tools are just some of the ways that you will get better results. In four cases by employing the inbuilt power of the mind's goal setting ability you'll get better results without consciously doing anything except by keeping the mind on your most important objectives.

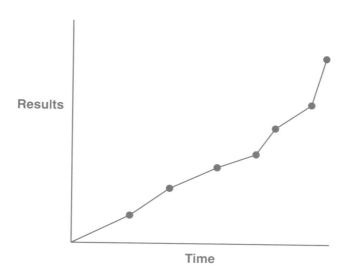

31.

10 Steps to Financial Independence

"Start saving now! The first £ makes the most money"

1. Start saving something **now.**
   (It always pays to save half as much for twice as long than twice as much for half as long.)

2. Put it where ideally you can't get at it.

3. Ideally, save 10% of your income.

4. **Save first.** That is deduct it from your income as you get it, and live on the balance.

5. Put the majority in no risk funds invested in equities and gilts, not banks or building societies.

6. Save further money in an accessible fund so that you can get at it when an emergency occurs allowing you to leave the bulk of your long term **10%** savings fund intact.

7. **Use all the tax breaks** open to you in full:
   a. Fully fund your pensions
   b. Fully fund your I.S.A's (in UK)

8. Don't rent money at the wrong rates. Review all your mortgage and loan interest rates. Where possible cut them.

9. Review the cost of your life assurances, health insurances and critical illness assurances. The price of these is going down as life expectancy extends. You will save money.

10. Don't be fooled into thinking your retirement won't last long. My guess is that from today onward you'll spend more time in retirement than you will at work. You will probably spend thirty years or more in retirement.
    You must save. The sooner you start the more you'll have.

32.

Towards Unlimited Wealth

"We're entering a golden age of unlimited prosperity"

Alchemy is the ancient science of turning base metal into gold. For a series of reasons we are set to see a form of economic alchemy in the next twenty years.

1. **USA Stock Market Set to Rise**

   The next few years to 2009 offer an extraordinary opportunity for us to create financial independence.

   Thanks to a baby boom in 1960 the year 2009 will see a peak in the number of 47 year old males. At 47 US males reach their peak spending power in the USA.

   Historically, any peak in male spending power has coincided with a high in the US stock market.

   The probability is that Dow Jones will rise to between **15,000** and **25,000** by **2009.**

   As **52%** of the world's stock market is in the USA this 'engine' will drive all other European markets and these markets will peak too around 2010 to 2012.

   Being invested in these markets **could** treble your money.

2. **Technology creates wealth without regard to any scarcity of resources**

   Remember too we are entering an age of abundance when consumer demand will be met by increasingly greater technological innovation. All owners of businesses that feed that need can become independently wealthy, and put more money into the world than has been seen before.

3.   **Age – life expectancy**

Since 1800 there isn't a single 10 year period where any other form of asset has exceeded the investment returns of the UK and UK stock markets. See statistics in the next section.

With people retiring around 60 and living until 85 to 90 some of their money will have to go in the stock market if it's to retain its buying power so extended life expectancy will fuel the markets too.

Conclusion

There are three reasons to believe we are entering a golden era the likes of which have not been seen before.

They are, again.

1.   Rising numbers of 47 year old males in the USA each year from 2002 to 2009.

2.   Technology manufactures solutions to consumer needs in a way that creates wealth for those doing it.

3.   Increasing life expectancy forces long term investors to look beyond banks, building societies, gilts and bonds to a higher performing class of asset, equities so money will go into these markets driving them higher.

These three reasons will make a lot of people exceptionally wealthy.

You have it within you to be one of them too. Start your savings programme for a fantastic future now!

33.

Towards Riches, The Power Of Stock Markets

Since 1871 in the USA and 1899 in the UK in any 10 year period stock markets outpace all other forms of investment on 84% and 92% of all occasions.

USA 82.1%

	Time Period	Bonds	Deposits
10 yrs	1871-1996	82.1%	84.6%

UK 86%

	Time Period	Bonds	Deposits
10 yrs	1899-2000	86%	92%

34.

21 Tips for Superb Good Health

"The body is the temple of the soul"

To excel at life you need zest, energy, zap, vitality. Remember you'll live 'til 80, 90, 100 or more so it's probably better to feel great not grotty or gross!

Here are 21 life extenders!

1. An annual health check.

2. Get a personal fitness and fat assessment at a gymnasium or health club.

3. Integrate fitness activities into your life.

4. Exercise at least 3 times a week so that your cardiovasular system is under moderate pressure. The goal is to be slightly out of breath so that the lungs have to work harder than usual after 20 minutes of sustained aerobic exercise.

5. Eat dinner and finish by 8.00 pm. Have 2-3 hours after you've eaten before going to bed. Late meals and sedentary lifestyles pile on the fat.

6. Look for low fat foods but not all fat is bad for you. Research indicates it's as important to restrict your carbohydrate input as it is to restrict your fat input.

7. Eat more organic vegetables and fruit, can you grow your own?

8. Drink plenty of water, at least 4 pints a day to flush through fats and impurities.

9. Take **Vitamin C, Vitamin E** and **natural Beta Carotene** every day.

10. If you are concerned about digestion, try taking **digestive enzyme additives.** Enzymes break down our food making it more easily digestible. All cooked food has its enzymes destroyed so digestion of these foods is harder. The body therefore has to provide the enzymes to ensure food is digested. The older you get the lower your enzyme 'bank balance' becomes so you need a supplement.

    Digestive enzyme additives aid digestion breaking down food into its constituent parts and releasing the nutrients the body needs more easily. **These really work.** For details of these please contact me, I'll be happy to help.

11. If you have breathing difficulties take '**Vitamin O**'. It's a form of stabilised oxygen. It helps at altitude, helps asthmatics and helps anyone having breathing difficulties.

12. If you drink, don't drink to excess – it'll damage your liver.

13. Don't smoke. It takes over 2 years to remove the effects of smoking from the lungs and it inhibits your ability to exercise freely, taste your food, and it'll cut down your dry cleaning bills!

14. Laugh every day!

15. Set a goal for your life span and think positively about your life expectancy.

16. Find new ways to exercise. Brisk walking, dancing, making love, horse riding, cycling, swimming, aerobics.

17. Find a quiet space in every day just to be, most of us should be called human doings rather than human beings, just be!

18. Weigh yourself weekly, set weight goals.

19. Take a paper bag cut two eyeholes, strip off and put the bag on your head. Your face has gone so it could be someone else. If you don't like what you see, take some action!

20. Be optimistic.

21. Stay in love!

35.

Goal Setting

This section is extracted from "The Sky Is Not The Limit", my book on goal setting.

There are 8 chapters here, the book itself contains 80 chapters plus 31 personal planning pages.

If this section is of interest, I strongly advise you to obtain a copy. It's completely transferable to people of all ages from 10-100 from all walks of life.

36.

Goals

"You set the goal and then you see, you do not see then set the goal"
Louis Tice

To go somewhere, we must know where somewhere is!

We wouldn't fly with a pilot who didn't have a destination. We wouldn't play a game of football without goal posts on the field. Equally, for personal achievement to work we must have specific destinations; meaningful objectives to achieve. This process is known as "goal setting".

We set goals in the six areas of our lives:

Financial
Business
Private
Social
Physical
Spiritual

The good news about setting and achieving goals is that we are **all** goal orientated and we have a built in goal setting mechanism.

Without consciously selecting any meaningful goals, we nevertheless go through our lives achieving them. Maslow, in his Theory of Hierarchical Needs, states that we strive automatically to fulfil five principle goals. These are the physiological, security, social, esteem, and self-fulfilment goals. All of us are able to achieve most of these needs because our mind has a built in goal seeking mechanism in which the conscious and subconscious minds combine to achieve our goals for us.

The conscious mind gives the instructions to the subconscious mind, and the subconscious mind seems to carry them out. Whatever the conscious mind asks of it, the subconscious seeks to achieve.

Remember the example we quoted earlier of how this looks.

The conscious mind passes the instructions, the subconscious seeks to carry them out.

If the hypnotist puts a subject under hypnosis he can then control their conscious mind and make the subject do all manner of things.

For example, he can indicate to somebody that he is going to place a red hot poker on the palm of the subject's hand. He will then take a pen or pencil, not a red hot poker, place it on the palm of the subject's hand and the subject will react as though the pen or pencil was a red hot poker. This works to such an extent that the skin could even blister.

The conscious mind reacts to the conditions it has been told exist by the hypnotist and passes the facts, about the red hot poker, directly to the subconscious mind which in turn seeks to fulfil the conditions consistent with a red hot poker being placed on the palm of the hand.

Because the subconscious thinks there is a red hot poker touching the palm of the hand, it seeks to fulfil the conditions it has been told exist.

We operate on our belief of the facts and not the facts themselves.

The human brain is a massive computer. Different programmes inserted into the brain will produce different outcomes.

We can programme our minds to accomplish whatever we truly want.

With the conscious mind controlled by the hypnotist, the subconscious mind seeks to fulfil whatever the conscious mind **believes** it should be achieving in that situation.

We are all achieving some of our goals now, most of the lower order Maslow goals are achieved by most people every day, because our computer, our brain, is intuitively programmed to programme their minds to do so. But most people do not consciously or deliberately programme their minds to achieve anything meaningful, so achieve nothing meaningful. They do not seek the self-fulfilment they truly desire because they don't know it's available to them.

Our brain is a computer and unless it is programmed to achieve new goals, will keep on achieving the old ones, re-running the old programmes like breathing, eating and sleeping, dressing appropriately, getting to the office on time, and so on. All perfectly acceptable, but not exactly exciting or fulfilling.

Part of the problem is that it is difficult for people to "breakout" and do the unusual. The "social" cost of not conforming with their peer group's expectations of them, is high.

Some people do break these "social" rules but most people would rather stay within their peer groups, rather than stand apart from them.

Yet it is precisely that which they have to do, to set goals, to reach for the unusual, to dare to win.

Goal setters and achievers cannot be part of the crowd and stand out from the crowd at the same time. Deciding what you want for yourself requires selfishness.

If you want to achieve the things you deep down really want to achieve, you have to choose to act for yourself. Step out from the majority, remembering that most of the majority, sadly, never achieve anything meaningful.

37.

Why Goal Setting Works

"Goals create focus"

We already achieve simple goals each day. If we substitute goals for the mundane ones, the mind will set about accomplishing them.

When we decide on something we'd really like, the mind acts as a magnet, attracting to it all the components necessary to accomplish the goal. This is easily demonstrated.

When you want to buy a new car, the newspapers are full of cars for sale, and you select one. When you don't want to buy a car the newspapers are still full of cars but you don't notice them because they are no longer important to you.

It is only when we set the goal that the information relevant to achieving it becomes more prominent.

Put another way, we set the goal and then we see, we do not see then set the goal.

The mind acts like a tape recorder, it is recording all we experience and how we feel about it. Yet our conscious mind cannot consciously cope with all the information it is being bombarded with, so it filters out what it doesn't need, leaving it to focus on only what it needs to achieve the goal.

When we set a goal we trigger a valuable filter in the brain. In flying, this system used to be known as a C.A.G. (Central Attention Getter). Our goal is a Central Attention Getter drawing to it the components necessary to achieve it. The brain begins to relate the normally unrelated, and things start to happen.

Because the brain filters out what is not important, it's the value of the information, not the amount that matters.

We must write down our goals and get them sharply focused, the clearer our picture, the more certain the possibility of our achieving it.

38.

Goal Setting Works

"Anything the mind of man can conceive and believe it can achieve"
Napoleon Hill

In a survey of students leaving their university in the U.S.A. in the 60's, they were asked if they had set any goals for their future. The survey showed that only 7% of them had their goals clearly written down.

Twenty years later, the same students were surveyed again and the 7% who had their goals clearly written down had achieved more in terms of wealth and success than the remaining 93%.

The Proof

Suppose that John is a sales manager and Jim is a salesman. If I am a redundant salesman with money in the bank, John might consider recruiting me because he wants a salesman.

Jim, on the other hand, would want to sell me a product because he only sells products.

John's goal, to recruit, is different from Jim's goal, to sell. I have a different value to John than I do to Jim, because John's goal is different from Jim's.

If Jim didn't have a goal to recruit, I would be of no value to him.

It is his goal that gives me a value.

You set the goal and then you see. You don't see then set the goal.

39.

Setting Goals - How

"Make no little plans: they have no magic to stir men's souls"
Daniel Burnham

We set goals in the six main areas of our lives:

Financial
Business
Social
Private
Physical
Spiritual

What exactly are your goals?

This is your opportunity to dream. You are going to require privacy, peace and quiet, plain paper and a pen and at least a couple of hours to yourself.

1.   Write them all down

Having arranged this, write down everything you'd really like to have, be, or achieve in life.

For example:
- **to own a large detached house with 3 acres of ground**
- **to play tennis well**
- **to be more patient**
- **to have £100,000 in savings**
- **to travel around the world**
- **to be a good after dinner speaker**

The list is as long as your imagination allows it!

Two Rules

When you write your goals down, follow two basic rules.

a. **Your goals are the things that you want.**

 Don't change them to conform with what you believe others might expect of you.

b. **Don't leave anything out.**

 Anything you'd like should be written down. Don't prejudge your ability to accomplish it. Write it down no matter how impossible it may seem at the time. Leave nothing out.

Five life changing questions

Ask yourself the following questions that I first heard Brian Tracy use, to get you to focus on what really counts.

a. **If you had 10 minutes to live, who would you call and what would you say?**
b. **If you had six months to live, how would you spend your time?**
c. **What five things do you value most in your life?**
d. **What are the three most important goals in your life right now?**
e. **What one thing would you attempt to do, if you knew you wouldn't fail?**

2. **Define each goal in detail**

Write each goal in specific terms. Expand each goal to include a detailed and precise description of what you seek.

For example:

 A large detached house with 3 acres of ground.

This becomes:

A large detached house with 3 acres in the country within 30 minutes journey time from the office. 3 reception rooms, 2 bathrooms, 4 bedrooms, study, 2 garages, kitchen, utility room, outbuildings to include a greenhouse and 2 stables.

For example:

 To play tennis well.

66

This becomes:

To be able to play competently at club level in both singles and doubles, to have had two dozen lessons, and to have got to the last sixteen in the club league.

These goals are **specific** not generalised.

3. Detail

The added detail helps you visualise the goal more clearly. The more you define it, the clearer it becomes. The clearer it becomes, the greater the likelihood you have of accomplishing it.

4. Priorities

Put each of the six goals listed in order of priority. Don't be concerned if some goals appear on more than one list, it happens.

5. Deadlines

A goal is meaningless without a deadline. The first goal on each list should have a deadline for accomplishment and if you have never really set goals before, that deadline should be no less than 2 months and no more than 6 months away.

6. Plan of Action

Take the first goal from each list and write down the actions that you think you will have to take to achieve it.

7. Obstacles

Write down all the obstacles that will prevent your goal being attained, then write down solutions in terms of the attitudes and actions you will have to adopt to overcome them.

Here is an example:

Physical Goal   Weight 12 stone 7 lbs by September 1 st
                           Present weight: 13 stone 9 lbs

Actions

>   Exercise – run or walk 2 miles 5 times a week
>   Diet – avoid butter, fatty meats, cheese
>   Weight loss – 8 weeks at 2 lbs a week

8. Affirmations state the goal in the present tense

If you state the goal in the present tense, it enters the subconscious from the conscious as though already achieved. This is deliberate. It makes the subconscious behave as if the goal is already attained, ensuring it behaves in a manner consistent with its accomplishment.

This "trick" of the mind gets the subconscious working on bringing about the change you desire. It brings the goal nearer, faster. You are conditioning your mind, **programming** your mind, to believe that the goal is achieved. This creation of a false belief in the subconscious creates the correct conditions for the subconscious mind to be in step with your conscious desire to attain the goal.

Use of present tense affirmations to reinforce your goal, that is, **"I am punctual"**, **"I am enthusiastic"**, **"I am successful"**, programmes the subconscious.

9. Actions

Carry out the steps of your action plan in the complete faith that they will come about. Remember winners have belief without evidence.

40.

Affirmations

"To be all that we can be, not just who we are"
John Denver

Your **Definite Chief Aim.** Once all the goals are set a specific pattern will emerge and a definite chief aim relating to your life, probably some five to ten years hence, will emerge.

Your **Definite Chief Aim** becomes the dominating drive for your five to ten year business plan and all your goals are subordinated to it and co-ordinated with it.

Your **Definite Chief Aim** is your specific purpose for the next five to ten years, it will give you the long term perspective necessary to overcome the short-term red traffic light obstacles that will inevitably occur.

41.

Goal Lists And Affirmations

"Goal setting is important, goal doing is more important"

Your goal list will look something like this:

My Personal Goals

1   **Weight 12 stone 7 lbs by 1st September 2002**
2   **To be more decisive in my business**
3   **To save £2,500 by Christmas 2002**
4   **To start work on my family tree this year**
5   **To earn promotion in my job by January 2003**

Signed: A Chiever   Dated: 1.5.2002

Your affirmations for these goals will look like this:

Affirmations

1   **I am 12 stone 7 lbs**
2   **I am decisive**
3   **I am saving £2,500 and will have it set aside by Christmas 2002**
4   **I am drawing up my family tree**

42.

Using Your Goal Lists and Affirmations

"One day is worth two tomorrow's, never leave that
'til tomorrow which you can do today"
Benjamin Franklin

To continually keep your goals in the forefront of your mind, you must keep copies of them, handwritten each time, dated and signed by you, where you will continually see them. For example, copies should be:

- In your wallet
- In your diary
- On your steering wheel
- On your bathroom mirror
- On your desk

These will act as a reinforcement each time you see them.

43.

Pictures

"Man's desires are limited by his perceptions,
none can desire what he has not perceived"
William Blake

The more clearly we see our goals, the more likely we are to achieve them. To make them "live" once you've set them, use pictures prominently displayed on your desk, in your study, in your diary, on your bedroom mirror to remind you of why you are striving to achieve your goals.

Get detailed pictures of your goals and surround yourself with them. The power of these pictures will reinforce your ability to achieve your goals. Visualise in your mind your circumstances when you've achieved your goal.

Take time to build a mental picture of the way life will be and how you'll feel when your goal is attained.

Picture your goals as though they were in your **possession** already. Visualisation makes your goals come to life.

44.

Personal Fulfilment

"Happiness is the by-product of accomplishing your goals in life"

Comes from deciding what you want from life then setting goals to achieve it.

Zig Ziglar says "You can get anything in life you want as long as you'll help other people get what they want."

Life isn't meant to be miserable. Personal goal setting is the key.
Meantime I'll leave you with a story.

"It wasn't difficult for a boy of 15 to make a list of everything he'd ever wanted. After all, he had a vivid imagination and an eye for detail so he sat and wrote out his list of personal goals, wrote the man of 62 as he crossed off his 92nd life goal."

Are you 40, 50, 60 and still unfulfilled?

There's a saying "Most men live lives of quiet desperation". It doesn't have to be that way.

So define your future by deciding what you'd ideally like it to contain. The clearer you define it the more certain the outcome.

The future **is** there for those who invent it.
As Stephen Covey says in his book "The 7 Habits of Highly Effective People" what are we here for?

"To live, to love, to learn, to leave a legacy"

So what's your legacy going to be? Don't let your music die inside you. Be all you can be - that's why you're alive!

45.

Anything's Possible!

Here again is the resume of the key facts contained in this book.

Eighteen Steps To Success

1. The world is changing but our values should not.
2. In a world of virtual reality, people will want real relationships.
3. If we give value then we have the right to income. If we give more value we have the right to more income.
4. Entrepreneurs control the future, as an entrepreneur you can assure your financial independence.
5. Technology is an aid to better practice, not a threat.
6. We do not have to work five times harder to achieve five times the result.
7. In an increasingly complex world we will all seek simplicity.
8. Busy people don't want more information, they want less information from a source they can trust.
9. We need to work on our business instead of constantly working in it.
10. We can't do that unless we delegate.
11. We need to understand the huge difference between being a 'determined one man band' and being part of a team of people with complimentary strengths.
12. Napoleon Hill's Mastermind principle confirms that 'the sum of the whole is greater than the contribution of the individual parts.'
13. Our methods of working need to change but our values should not.
14. We must delegate what we are not good at to do what we know will give us our biggest pay-off.
15. To delegate we have to 'let go of the edge', and trust our intuition and instincts to give us the result we seek.
16. The decision to let go is usually made without the supporting evidence to prove it will work when we do let go.

17. Winners have belief without evidence, the mediocre need evidence before they believe.

18. Our biggest pay-off is when our unique skill is employed on our most valuable opportunity. We must reposition our business to guarantee that that happens.